A Family in China

LIBRARY OF CONGRESS CATALOGING IN PUBLICATION DATA

Fyson, Nance Lui
  A family in China.

  Previously published: Chun Ling in China.
  Summary: Describes the life of a twelve-year-old from
rural northeast China and the ways her life is different
from when her mother was a child.
  1. Communes (China)—Juvenile literature. 2. China—
Social life and customs—1976-   —Juvenile literature.
[1. China—Social life and customs] I. Greenhill,
Richard, ill. II. Title.
HD1492,C5F97 1985   306'.0951   84-19426
ISBN 0-8225-1653-5 (lib. bdg.)

Manufactured in the United States of America

2 3 4 5 6 7 8 9 10 94 93 92 91 90 89 88

A Family in China

Nance Lui Fyson and Richard Greenhill

Lerner Publications Company · Minneapolis

Wang Chun Ling is 12 years old and lives in the Liaoning (lee ow ning) province in China. Like three out of every four Chinese people, she lives in the countryside.

China is the third largest country in the world in land area. Only Russia and Canada are bigger. Wang Chun Ling has never seen most of her country and would be surprised to hear that nearly a quarter of all the people in the world live in China!

Where Wang Chun Ling lives the summers are hot and the winters are very cold. These pictures of her were taken in July. In the winter she wears layers of padded cotton clothes to keep warm. Even her winter shoes are made of padded cotton.

Russia

Pakistan

India

C H

Tibet

Mount Everest

Nepal

Bhutan

Wang Chun Ling lives in a group of houses with nearly 200 people. This group is called a production team. Many of the people in the production team are her relatives.

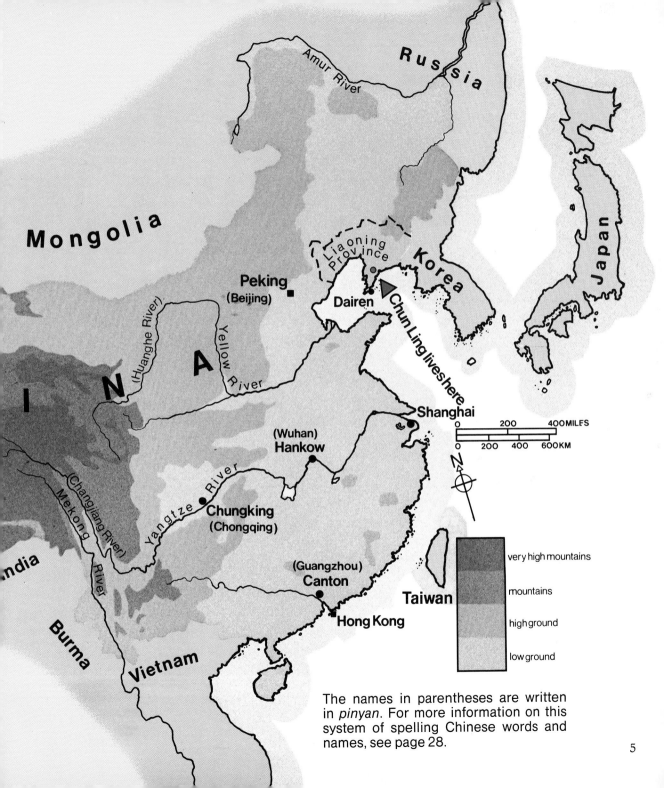

R u s s i a

Amur River

Mongolia

Japan

Peking
(Beijing)

Liaoning
Province

Korea

Dairen

Chun Ling lives here

(Huanghe River)

Yellow River

I N A

Shanghai

0   200   400 MILES

0   200   400   600 KM

(Wuhan)
Hankow

N

(Changjiang River)

Yangtze River

Chungking
(Chongqing)

Mekong River

(Guangzhou)
Canton

Taiwan

ndia

Burma

Vietnam

Hong Kong

very high mountains

mountains

high ground

low ground

The names in parentheses are written
in *pinyan*. For more information on this
system of spelling Chinese words and
names, see page 28.

5

Wang Chun Ling is standing with some of her family by their house. Nearly one-third of what the family earns comes from selling food grown in the garden near the house.

The family also earns money and food by working on large pieces of land which belong to every-one. The land is divided among communes. A commune is a group of thousands of people who own and work the land together. Each commune is broken up into smaller production teams like Wang Chun Ling's.

People also share most of the animals. It is common to see chickens wandering around the courtyards between the houses. In the courtyards, people meet and chat, hang up washing, and boil water in big black kettles for tea. There is one water faucet which everyone shares. Wang Chun Ling's house does not have a water faucet.

The courtyard is also a good place to chop food. The family eats mainly noodles, rice, and steamed bread rolls with such vegetables as beans, onions, cabbage, and mushrooms. They also eat eggs, fish, and some meat. Dried seaweed is popular, and so are apples.

7

The kitchen inside Wang Chun Ling's house is in the center, with one room on each side. The whole family sleeps together on large raised brick platforms called *kangs*. Straw mats and quilts are put over the bricks. When the weather is cold, fires are lit beneath the *kangs* to keep everyone warm.

Wang Chun Ling's family also sits on a *kang* to eat. They eat with chopsticks. Her father is called Wang Ji Wu and her mother is Chang Gu Zhi. Chun Ling has her father's surname of Wang and will keep this all her life. Women don't change their names when they marry.

Most of the food that Wang Chun Ling eats comes from the commune. Some kinds of food are rationed in China. You need both coupons and money to buy that food, and you can't always buy as much as you want. Many people in China are poorer than Wang Chun Ling and her family, but most do have enough to eat.

9

There is one television set in Wang Chun Ling's group of houses. About 25 families watch it. As farm peasants, Wang Chun Ling's parents would have to save all their earnings for a year to buy their own TV.

When Wang Chun Ling was younger, people saved up to buy bicycles, watches, and radios. Bicycles are important for getting around. In China, there are buses but very few private cars. To buy a car, a worker would have to save everything he or she earned for about 18 years!

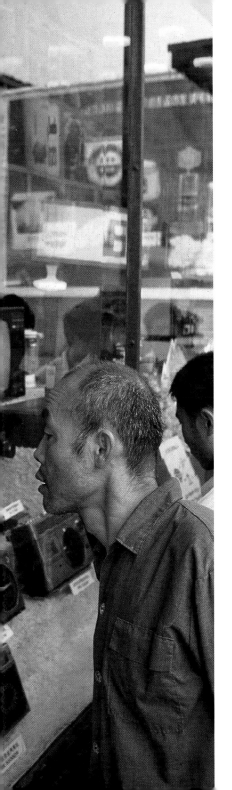

In each family, several people earn money. Women do every kind of job that men do, so families can save and buy some of the goods that have become available only recently in China. But Wang Chun Ling's family still has much less money to spend than families that live in North America, Australia, or Europe.

The commune has shops like the one shown here, small factories, a clinic or hospital, and day-care centers where small children are looked after while their parents work.

About two-thirds of the Chinese working people are farmworkers like Wang Chun Ling's family. Many of their tools are made of wood, and they have a few simple metal tools like hoes and sickle blades. There are very few machines.

It is mostly human energy that does the work on the farms. Water buffalo help by pulling plows, but much of the land is too dry or hilly to be farmed easily. Only about one-ninth of the land is used for growing crops.

Because there are so many people to feed in China, the Chinese use every bit of land they can. People even grow food by the sides of the roads and next to railroad tracks.

The Chinese are also careful not to waste any leftover scraps of food. People in the cities save scraps which are sent out to the countryside to feed pigs. Pigs are the most common farm animal and are kept in piggeries like the one in the picture. Pig dung is very good for putting on the fields to make the crops grow better.

Cats and dogs are working animals in China. They help to catch mice and rats. For pets, the Chinese are fond of goldfish and caged birds.

Wang Chun Ling helps look after all the animals on the farm. She catches ducks and geese when they are going to be cooked. She also chops firewood.

In rural China, most children go to primary school from ages 6 to 11. There are very few secondary schools, and Wang Chun Ling is very lucky to be going to one. Only about one-third of the children in China go on to secondary school.

School codes say children must not swear or fight and must study hard. They should love their country, respect their teachers, be polite to others, be modest and honest, and love physical work. Included in secondary schools are factory units where young people help to make such things as parts for radios.

It is hard for a poor country like China to give everyone a full education. The primary schools are crowded, with about 50 children in each class. In some of the classes there are only a few books and posters, and students must learn almost everything by listening to the teacher. Neither primary nor secondary education is free. Each family must pay to send its children to school.

Wang Chun Ling's mother and father didn't go to school at all. Like many adults in rural China, they can't read or write. But children learn a lot from these adults. Old people live with their families and are greatly loved and respected.

Wang Chun Ling has told her parents and grandparents about the English she has learned in school. She is also learning to read and write Chinese. Good handwriting is very important in China. One Chinese saying can be translated as "Handwriting is the face of you." This means that what kind of person you are will be shown by the way you write.

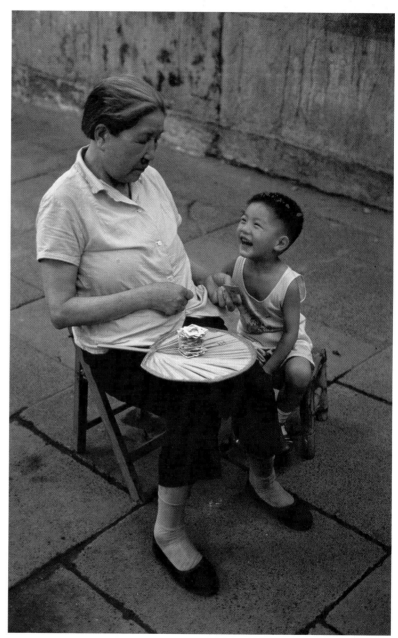

Chinese characters are almost like pictures. The character for "people" is 人. It almost looks like a person.

Children in primary school learn characters such as

大　小　多　少　上　下　来　去

big　small　more　less　up　down　come　go

Adults need to know over 3,000 characters just to read a newspaper. Experts know more than 5,000 characters.

"Wǒ jiào (war jow) Wang Chun Ling" means "My name is Wang Chun Ling."

This is how Wang Chun Ling says "How are you?":

"Nǐ hǎo (nee how)?"

An address on a letter being sent to China looks like this:

Wang Chun Ling has cousins who live in Shanghai, a big city. They go to Children's Palaces after school for activities. There aren't any Children's Palaces in the countryside where Wang Chun Ling lives. She would love the chance to go to one.

The Children's Palaces are centers where children learn to play musical instruments, make puppets, paint, and perform songs and dances. There are also games like those at a fairground.

Children come to the centers for free. But they must be chosen for some of the activities. The most musical children may learn to play the violin and piano. Chinese instruments like the pipa are popular.

Some children build radios and do science experiments. The Palaces also show science work done in classrooms, so children can see what has been done in other schools. There are competitions among schools in subjects like mathematics.

Children in both the city and the country play outside after school. A favorite game is "five stones," which is like jacks. Marbles and soccer are also popular.

Wang Chun Ling and her friends enjoy skipping rope. Another favorite game is "kick bag." Six pieces of cloth are sewn together to make a little bag and grain or sand is put inside. Children kick the bag to keep it in the air.

The children also play a game called *ti jian zi.* Old copper coins, no longer used as money, have holes in the center. A feather is put tightly through the holes, and the children kick the coins, trying to keep them in the air. (*Ti* means "to kick.")

Ping pong is a very popular game with both adults and children. The tables are often made of cement, and a line of bricks is used in place of a net.

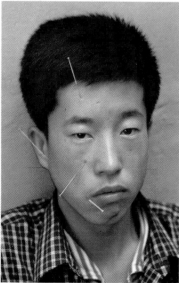

Wang Chun Ling also enjoys card games. Like these children, she played cards in the hospital when she was ill.

Sick people are often treated in China by acupuncture. This boy has acupuncture needles sticking into his face to make him feel better. Because the needles are very thin, they don't hurt. They are put into the body at special places, depending on what is wrong. The needles can also stop pain during an operation. Acupuncture has been used in China for thousands of years. Plant medicines are also used to treat the sick.

There are few fully trained doctors in the area where Wang Chun Ling lives. "Barefoot doctors," like the man shown here, help out. They have enough training to cure everyday problems and have been given this name because they share the simple life of the people they help. They do not really work with bare feet, but wear shoes or sandals. Wang Chun Ling's farmer neighbor is a barefoot doctor for their group of houses.

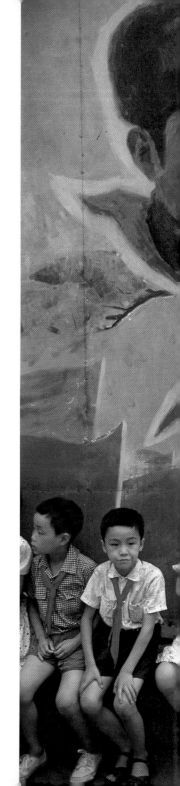

Better health care is only one of many changes in China since Wang Chun Ling's mother was a child. There have also been many changes in the 12 years since Wang Chun Ling was born.

When Chun Ling was small, women wore only blue or gray cotton suits with loose trousers and jackets buttoned up to the neck. Now some women wear colorful scarves and simple cotton dresses and skirts. Some women even wear makeup and curl their hair. Billboards in the cities advertise many products.

China now has free markets as well as state markets. At the free markets, farmers can sell what they have grown on their own small plot of land.

The Chinese have learned to share and work together for the good of everyone. But now what each person wants is also becoming important. What will China be like when Wang Chun Ling is old?

The Chinese Language 汉字

Instead of an alphabet, the Chinese writing system uses characters to represent words. You have already seen some characters on page 19, including the Chinese character for "people." Three other words that build on the same character are shown below. Can you see the similarity?

人　　　仁　　　体　　　他
people　　humane　　body　　he/him

Because the sounds in the Chinese language are different from those in English, it is difficult to write down the Chinese sounds using the alphabet we know. Two main systems have been invented to do this. In the older system, called Wade-Giles, the capital city of China is spelled Peking. In pinyan, the newer system, the capital is spelled Beijing. The Chinese write the same word like this:

北京

In 1979, the government of the People's Republic of China requested that all Chinese words and names appearing in English be written in pinyan. You'll find both systems used on the map on pages 4 and 5.

Facts about China

Capital: Beijing (Peking)

Language: many dialects of Chinese

The Northern dialect, *p'u-t'ung hua* (sometimes called Mandarin Chinese), is the official language of the country.

Form of Money: the yuan

Area: 3,678,470 square miles (9,527,200 square kilometers)

This area is slightly larger than the area of the United States, including Alaska and Hawaii. China is the third largest country in the world, and the United States ranks fourth.

Population: about 1,097,000,000 people

About five times as many people live in China as live in the United States.

NORTH
AMERICA

SOUTH
AMERICA

EUROPE

A S I A

China

AFRICA

AUSTRALIA

Families the World Over

Some children in foreign countries live like you do. Others live very differently. In these books, you can meet children from all over the world. You'll learn about their games and schools, their families and friends, and what it's like to grow up in a faraway land.

Lerner Publications Company, 241 First Avenue North, Minneapolis, Minnesota 55401